Take a trip to

HAITI

John Griffiths

Franklin Watts

London   New York   Sydney   Toronto

Facts about Haiti

Area:
27,750 sq. km.
(10,715 sq. miles)

Population:
6,187,000 (1987)

Capital:
Port-au-Prince

Largest Cities:
Port-au-Prince (473,000)
Cap Haïtien (72,000)
Gonaives (37,000)
Les Cayes (36,000)

Official languages:
French and Creole

Religion:
Christianity, Voodoo

Main Exports:
Coffee

Currency:
Gourde

Franklin Watts
96 Leonard Street
London EC2A 4RH

Franklin Watts Inc.
387 Park Avenue South
New York, N.Y. 10016

ISBN: UK Edition 0 86313 968 X
ISBN: US Edition 0-531-10735-3
Library of Congress Catalog Card No:
89-8940

© Franklin Watts Limited 1989

Typeset by Lineage, Watford
Printed in Hong Kong

Maps: Simon Roulstone
Design: K & Co

Front Cover: ZEFA
Back Cover: ZEFA

Photographs: Pablo Butcher 4, 5, 9, 13;
J Allen Cash 26, 27; J Griffiths 17, 31;
Hutchinson Library 6, 12, 16, 18, 22, 24,
28, 29; MacQuitty International 15, 19;
Frank Spooner 14, 20, 23; Travel Photo
International 3, 8, 21; TROPIX 7; ZEFA
25, 30.

Stamps: Chris Fairclough

The Republic of Haiti makes up the western third of the island of Hispaniola in the Caribbean Sea. The Dominican Republic occupies the rest of the island. Haiti was once a French colony called Saint Dominigue. Haiti means 'land of mountains'.

When the explorer Christopher Columbus landed on Hispaniola, the island probably contained as many as 500,000 Taino Indians. By 1542, less than 500 remained. They were killed off by overwork, ill-treatment, and diseases brought from Europe.

   The Spaniards were the first to
import slaves from Africa in the 1520s.
Huge numbers of slaves were imported
by the French after they took over the
country in 1697 to work on the vast
sugar, coffee and cotton plantations.

The French Revolution of 1789 sparked the revolution which ended French rule of Saint Dominigue. A slave revolt began in 1791 led by Toussaint L'Ouverture. The rebels were finally victorious in 1804.

After independence, the slaves set up their own small farms. They cleared forests in their search for land and fuel. With the removal of the trees, the rain washed away the exposed soil. Today soil erosion is a severe problem in Haiti.

Haiti is a mountainous country. In the north, the mountains extend into the Dominican Republic and provide a natural barrier between the two countries. Pic la Selle, the highest peak, reaches 2677m (8,783 ft). Haiti's major river is the River Artibonite.

Haiti has a hot tropical climate. But the weather in mountains is much cooler than that on the coast. Hurricanes sometimes occur in summer. Earth tremors are common in the south.

The picture shows some stamps and
money used in Haiti. The main unit of
currency is the gourde, which is
divided into 100 centimes.

WORLD MAP

HAITI

Atlantic Ocean

CUBA

Windward Passage

Tortuga Island

Port-de-Paix

Cap Häitien

Gonaïves

Gulf of Gonâve

St Marc

HAITI

DOMINICAN REPUBLIC

Jérémie

Gonâve Island

Port-au-Prince

Les Cayes

Jacmel

Vache Island

Caribbean Sea

11

Most Haitians are either of African descent or are Mulattos (people of mixed African and European origin). They are the descendants of slaves. After 1804, few Europeans remained, though doctors, teachers and priests continued to work there.

Until 1988 the official language of
Haiti was French. But only 10 per cent
of the population spoke it. The
Constitution of 1988 also made Creole,
which most people speak, an official
language. The National Assembly
which produced the new Constitution
was elected in 1988.

Francois Duvalier, who was known as "Papa Doc", ruled Haiti as a dictator from 1957 to 1971. He did little to improve the conditions of life for most Haitians. Jean-Claude Duvalier, or "Baby Doc" (pictured above), succeeded his father in 1971. He was forced out of office in 1986.

The Duvaliers used priests called houngans, of the popular religion Voodoo to provide information and support. Although Roman Catholicism is the official religion of Haiti, most people believe in Voodoo as well.

Voodoo is important in the lives of Haitian people. It was taken to the Caribbean from West Africa by slaves transported by the French. At first it helped to give support to people who were taken from their own cultures and denied basic human rights.

Several religious groups, largely
funded by the United States, operate in
and around Port-au-Prince. The
picture shows the Baptist Mission at
Kenscoff. It runs schools and provides
medical and horiticultural services as
well as religious worship.

Port-au-Prince is Haiti's capital city. It is also a thriving port. More than 250,000 of its citizens live in appalling conditions in shanty towns. The rich live in the hills above the city.

Port-au-Prince differs greatly from the rest of the country. Three-quarters of all medical services, secondary schools and government services are based in the capital, as also are 90 per cent of all industrial jobs. There are few services such as schools and doctors, for people outside the capital.

Port-au-Prince has elaborately decorated buses, called "Tap-Taps". Most of them are owned by their drivers. The drivers keep them free of scratches through constant repainting and improvement of the designs.

Cap-Haitien, on the north coast, was a stronghold of the French after the slave uprising led by Toussaint L'Ouverture. It is built from, and on, the ruins of the city destroyed in 1802. "Le Cap", as Haitians call it, is now one of Haiti's more attractive cities.

Jeremie is one of the larger towns in
Haiti. It lies more than a day's travel
from Port-au-Prince, in the South-East
of the country. Travel is quite difficult
in Haiti although new roads have been
built recently to improve this. Jeremie
has many old colonial houses and is
the main market town for the region.

Since "Baby Doc" was ousted in February 1986, Haiti has been seeking a new kind of government. The military leaders have provided much of the country's leadership since 1986. The Church has also emerged as an important force.

Farming employs about 70 per cent of all workers. Most farms are small and produce hardly enough food for the farmer's family. The chief farm export is coffee. In 1980, a hurricane destroyed more than half of the coffee crop.

Sugar was the chief crop of the old French colonists. Since 1984, Haiti has not exported any sugar. Farmers face many problems, including drought, lack of irrigation, and low prices. Because of these problems, large amounts of food must be imported.

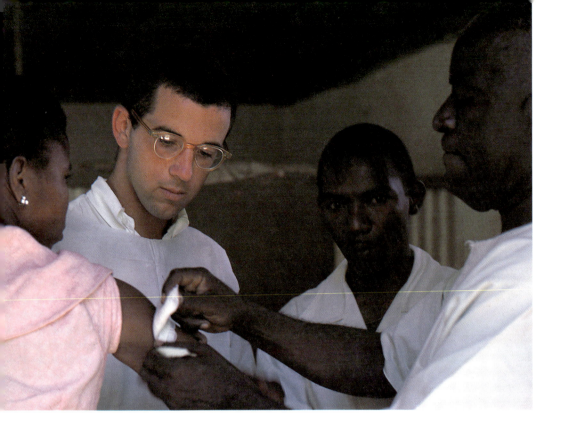

The health provision in Haiti is appalling and shows no signs of improving. One in three children dies before the age of five. Four out of five suffer from malaria. Health care in the countryside is almost entirely provided by charities and international agencies.

Educational services are also in short supply. The government runs some primary and secondary schools, and a university. There are also private schools, run largely by churches. But few schools exist in the countryside. Four out of every five people in Haiti cannot read or write.

Industries, such as food processing, textiles, and construction, are found mainly in the capital. From the 1970s, a growing number of small manufacturing and assembly industries, owned by the United States companies, have taken advantage of Haiti's cheap labour.

Fishing is an important source of income for many Haitians. Most fishing is done by one or two men in small boats called snail boats. Red snapper are caught, amongst other fish. The catch is taken to the local markets in woven baskets.

Huge carnivals are held on important religious occasions throughout the year, such as Easter week. The lively dancing and music have a strong Voodoo influence. The costumes are highly decorated.

The history of neglect in Haiti makes it difficult to be hopeful about the country's future. Many people sit daily outside the Cathedral in Port-au-Prince waiting for a miracle. The future desired by many Haitians after the fall of the Duvaliers in 1986 still appears to be a dream.

Index